Fuck Your Options!

a Christian Story

by

Larry A. Yff

TABLE OF CONTENTS

Introduction **3**

Christians and Options **5**

Private Matter Bonus Essays **39**

INTRODUCTION

Options aren't what they're cracked up to be and this is especially true if you are a Christian! In my book, "The Christian Who Didn't Give a Fuck", I gave you readers a brief introduction into how strongly I feel about all things God, the Bible and the Lost Books of the Bible...this book takes it a step further.

I felt it was necessary to help all of you Christians and so-called "Believers" out there simplify your life. Rules and laws make that possible.

For example, when you drive down the highway, you don't have to try and figure out what your maximum speed is. There is only one option because the law lets you know with posted signs: "70 mph maximum speed limit" or whatever the speed limit is on the highway in your State.

That's how the Bible works: follow the rules and laws God laid out for you and you should find success everywhere you go and in every area of your life! It's just that simple.

Anyways, you may have noticed the subtitle says "a Christian Story" and I used that for a reason: if you're claiming to be a Christian…YOUR OPTIONS DON'T MEAN SHIT and I'll tell you why…

CHRISTIANS and OPTIONS

Before we get started, I do want to clear up one other, itsy-bitsy point. In the beginning I put the term "Believers" in quotation marks. I did that because that term opens Christianity up to a whole lot of trickery and ambiguity. Not sure what "ambiguity" means? It's just a fancy word I like to throw around that basically means "confusing as fuck".

I'm a Christian...not a Believer. What in the fuck is a Believer anyways? Are you cocky enough to assume that by calling yourself a Believer the entire world knows what you believe in? Here's my take on it and then we'll get back into the book...

I know Christianity has a bad reputation and people who claim to be Christians are mixed about it. On one hand, they love being Christians, but on the other hand, they don't want to be associated with all the churchy scandals, hypocrisy, 2-facedness and a bunch of other shit associated with the church and I don't blame you BUT...when you take on a different title, it's as though you're throwing the baby out with the bathwater. Let me explain...

Being a Christian is a good thing. It's a respectable thing and to me it's the only thing. I fell for the bait and started telling people I was a Believer as well because it distanced me from the church and those messy-ass Christians. The only problem was, in doing so, I was telling people I believed in something and that something has nothing to do with Christianity and all things God and that's not what I wanted to portray.

Remember I said, "...throw the baby out with the bathwater?" Well, that's a term that refers to the days when people lived in houses and only had enough water to bathe once a day and had very little gas to heat the water so everybody had to take a bath in the same tub, with the adults and older children going 1st.

After all these grown-ass people washed their asses, you can imagine what the bathwater usually looked like by the time it was the baby's turn to take a bath. Regardless of how dirty the water was though, the baby still needed to take a bath and no matter how dirty his ass still was…you can't just throw it and the water out! You still gotta take what's good out, and in this case it's the dirty baby, and get rid of the other shit which is the dirty water. Here's how that relates to what I was saying about being a "Believer" …

Christianity is about as pure of a spiritual path as you can take. I mean, when people want to try and criticize a religion or spiritual walk, they target Christians and Christianity. Nobody gives a fuck about the Amish, Buddhists, Mormons or any other off-brand religion…it's Christianity that has the bullseye on its' back.

You may be wondering why that is and I can only tell you my view and my view is that it's about as pure of a spiritual path as you can take and that's important. Nowadays, people are so sick of knowing the pastors are getting in trouble left and right for banging their church secretaries and the catholic church has 100 lawyers on retainer to handle all the cases where priests have gotten caught banging their alter-boys that religion is becoming quite the shit-show BUT...BUT regardless of all the riff-raff *inside* the church in general, Christianity as a religion and what it stands for is 100% the shit! It's the truth! It's thebomb.com!

Why is it so important that I clear all that up? It's important because, like I said earlier, I don't want you to miss out on all the good sex, money and happiness the Bible has for you just because *some* pastors and priests can't keep their dicks in their pants.

I don't want you to metaphorically "throw out the baby with the bathwater".

I don't want you to throw away all of the good shit Christianity offers you just because throughout humanity, humans have tried to use religion to manipulate the masses for their own gain and made religions in general look like they're all full of shit because actually they're not.

I know I said nobody gives a shit about Buddhists, people claiming to be Buddhists (We might get into that later, but it seems like all of a sudden everybody who has their hair in braids and likes candles, world peace, meditation, chimes and good marijuana is claiming to be a Buddhist...), the Amish and the Mormons, but I was slightly joking.

The point I was making with that statement was everybody around the world has something to say about Christianity and it's usually not good. Think I'm lying??? Okay, here's a little test with some questions:

1. What do you know about Mormons? Is it true you can have as many wives as you want? Is it true they believe their leader was inspired by God to rewrite the Bible and put it in his own words?

2. How about the Amish? Is it true they don't know how to use cellphones, aren't allowed to get haircuts, don't drink or smoke or use deodorant?

3. How about Buddhists? Can you tell me how many legs and arms Buddha has and whether or not he created the universe? Has anybody ever claimed to have seen this Buddha in real life?

4. What about Christianity? Is it true Christians claim Jesus died and rose from the dead 3 days later? Is the constitution of Christianity the Bible? How did Jesus die? How many days did it take for God to create the universe?

If I was a gambling man, which I am, I would bet you the average person reading this book has no ideal what those limbs are protruding from Buddha's body or if he ever claimed to have created the universe and if he did, I'll bet you don't know how many days it took.

I can run down the line for the examples I gave about the other religions and you, Average Reader, probably know about as much about the Amish and Mormons as I know the answer to the question, "Why are your chances of being elected President of the United States increased by 1,000% if you're a white male over the age of 83 with a bad hairdo and horrible fashion sense?"

On the flipside, I'll bet you dollars to donuts…hold on. Let me quickly tell you what that means. It means I'm so sure I'm right that if you bet me and put up 1,000 donuts, I would put up $1,000 dollars against your 1,000 donuts. See the image and the surety of what I'm about to say next? Good. Let's not stay here…

Christianity is a religion everybody knows about. I didn't say it was a religion everybody loves and I won't make that claim; however, I will say everybody has at least heard or understood at least 1, possibly 2 or 3, aspects about Christianity and that's something I think no other religion can safely say. Let's see...

1. I'll bet everybody has heard Christians believe in God
2. I'll bet everybody has heard Jesus is attached to Christianity
3. I'll bet everybody has heard the Virgin Mary is the mother of Jesus
4. I'll bet everybody has heard Christianity is attached to Heaven and Hell
5. I'll bet everybody has heard about Adam, Eve and the garden of Eden
6. I'll bet everybody has heard about Noah's Ark
7. I'll bet everybody has heard Christmas is attached to Christianity

So, how'd I do? Was I right? Do you agree that most people on the planet can admit they have heard about at least one of the 7 points I made regarding Christianity? I'm thinking I am right, Reader, so where's my 1,000 donuts that I won in the bet?

I'm not saying all of that to brag. I'm mentioning all of that to let you know that people have heard about Christianity. People have heard about God and Jesus. People have heard about all of those things BUT that doesn't mean people believe in all of those things and that's where we're gonna change gears and talk about another issue and that issue is what the book is all about: **as a Christian your options don't mean shit as it relates to everyday life!**

It is my honest opinion that 99% of people who don't respect Christianity is because of Christians. Yup. When you look at how Christians are living...why would you want to live like them? I'll also bet you that if Christians started taking all of their man-made options out of life, they would be happier, wealthier and more people would be able to benefit from the lifestyle the rules in the Bible that instruct us on how to live offers us. Let's see…

"God said He was gonna open the doors of Heaven and pour me out a blessing!!!" Really? Well, He did say that, but *why* did He say that? Do you know why in the fuck you're so happy about this point? I'm thinking if you as a Christian really knew what was behind the scenes of "opening the doors of Heaven and pouring you out so many blessings you won't be able to handle it", you may not be so happy.

If you read around that Bible verse you will notice God did in fact say He would pour out so many blessings from Heaven that it would make your head spin BUT in order to receive that, **you 1st have to bring your full tithe to Him.** Sounds simple, right?

You're ready for all God's blessings so all you have to do is take 10% of your paycheck and bring it to the church. What?!? Yeah. Tithe means 10%. If you had read the full verse, you would see that what God really said was, "...if you bring your full tithe to Me THEN I will pour out so many blessings..."

Are you still happy? Do you still want all those blessings? I think a better question is: are you ready to give God 10% of your income? Oooweee! Do you know what that looks like? Let's take a quick look into it...

You get paid and now you, as a Christian, are supposed to tithe, so every Sunday when the collection plate comes around, you make sure you drop a 20-dollar bill in the plate and you're feeling good! Some of you may even drop a 50-dollar bill in the plate!

Quick question for you: is what you put in the plate equal to 10% of your gross paycheck? Based on the 2 examples I just gave you, if you put $20 in the plate, that would mean you had a gross paycheck (pre-tax) of $200. In the same vein, if you dropped that crispy 50-dollar bill in the plate, that means you grossed (pre-tax) $500.

How did you do? If you gave properly according to those calculations, you should be pretty happy! You should be happy for several reasons:

The 1st reason is that yes, you gave your full tithe to God and you should be receiving so many blessings from Heaven that you can't keep track of it all!

The 2nd reason why you should be pretty happy is you didn't decide to do what you felt like doing and exercise your option to put in the plate whatever you felt like putting in the plate.

Why am I bringing this up? Simple. I'm bringing it up because God is telling everybody who is a Christian one thing they can do to have wealth, health and whatever blessings God has to offer us that are both spiritual and physical. That's good news, right? NO!

That's horrible news for 99.9% of Christians around the world! It's horrible news because for 1, most of us have decided we have options. We have decided we have the option to decide what our tithe will be. We have decided to exercise our option of determining, based on our personal and corporate financial spreadsheets, what *we* think is a good amount to tithe...and the shit ain't working.

I'm saying it's not working and you can see it everywhere you look. If you're a Christian and are giving your full tithe, you should be walking and driving with a permanent smile on your face! You should be driving what ever car you want or walking in what ever shoes you decided to buy and you should be doing all of that with a big-ass smile on your face.

Why? Because you paid your full tithe and believed in God and His Word and did what you were supposed to do so God did what He was supposed to do.

Quick questions for you: How many of you have seen Christians who are broke as fuck? How many of you have seen churches that are rundown and raggedy-looking and in need of desperate repair? How many of you have heard Christians complaining about their finances?

If Christians are really supposed to be the "light of the world" and the "salt of the Earth" like Jesus said, they need to be blessed so they can be a blessing wherever they go. When a non-believer sees you coming, they should start getting butterflies of anticipation because they don't know how you're gonna bless them next!

Is that happening in the world today? Are "Christians" being a blessing? Are they happy with their financial situations?

Are they constantly in good health? If they were driving down a Michigan road and hit a Michigan-pothole and got a flat tire, were they able to fork over the dough to buy a new tire on the spot or were they cussing and calling their friends and family to let them borrow some money 'till payday to get their tire fixed?

Let me let you in on a little secret of mine. You ready? Come a little closer...closer...I KNOW ABOUT TITHING BECAUSE I DIDN'T TITHE WHAT I WAS SUPPOSED TO AND MY FINANCES WERE CONSTANTLY FUCKED UP UNTIL...UNTIL I STARTED TITHING THE FULL 10%!

See? I'm not here to bash the church or my fellow Christians. I'm here to share with you what I can from my experiences so you won't fall into the same pitfalls I did. I was telling people about all the good things God has in store for us and that you should follow God so "He can bless you with so much you won't be able to stand it!" meanwhile, I was broke, busted and disgusted!

Now, my situation is different than yours. All of our situations will be different but the positive results of following God's laws can still be the same regardless. In my situation, my finances weren't just leaving me because I wasn't tithing. For me, I wasn't getting all of my blessings for multiple reasons, all of which can be traced back to me and my "options". Wanna hear my sob story, Reader? Okay, here it is...

I thought as a Christian I had the option to have sex with whoever I wanted, but I didn't. God's laws clearly state a whole lot of laws about sex and I clearly didn't follow any of them like I was supposed to and my life reflected it.

Well, I did follow His law that says sex is for a man and a woman. Other than that, I made a mess of my life based on my sexual options.

If I had followed God's laws on sex, I would have gotten married, had a family and would have been there for them in every way every day of the week. Instead, I didn't get married and I wasn't able to take care of any of my children any day of the week.

1. I have multiple kids by multiple women
2. I went to jail *at least* 10 times for child-support related issues
3. I had my license suspended *at least* 10 times for child-support related issues
4. At least 1 of my older children expressed he or she (to protect his or her identity…not to go along with the whole "I can be a man or woman thing") didn't view me as a dad and basically didn't care and that's just the problems I was having as it related to my kids that could have easily been avoided. Let's continue with the list…
5. I was sleeping with a woman in a relationship and had to almost jump out a 4-story window on to my

car parked below to avoid getting caught when he came home earlier than expected (long story...)

6. I was involved in killing 2 of my children through abortions

7. I got hooked on porn because real sex for me had become a nightmare. This addiction even led me to looking at child porn. Since I felt guilty about my thoughts, I also had a cocaine addiction that fueled my sexual fantasy/porn addiction and I don't need to go into all the details on how smoking crack and sniffing coke are bad for you...

Do you see what I'm saying about exercising my sexual options? My options regarding sex don't mean shit! I'm a Christian so I'm supposed to be following God's laws on sex and I wasn't and my life reflected it.

What kind of example was I being about Christianity? A shitty one! Anybody who was thinking about Christianity and came across me knowing I was a Christian would have *definitely* given Christianity the middle finger! Let's talk some more about sex and options…

Before we go there, I have to add the silver lining to the cloud of shit that I put out there when I wasn't following God's laws.

I had begun to see all the chaos, confusion and depression in my life and wanted something more. I got that something more, and this is what I'm sharing with you, as I began to follow God's laws and stopped using my options:

1. I got married and started having good sex the way God designed it and that includes us using sex to have babies and create families.
2. I realized what my dick and sperm was designed for and stopped wasting time with porn.

3. I began to pray the daily Lord's Prayer like Jesus said every morning and that helped me fully recover from my cocaine addiction because I didn't want to be high and miss out on the plans God had for me for that day.
4. I began to tithe the full 10% to my church based on ANY gross income I make and as I've regularly done this, God has begun to download plans to me that are designed to create massive wealth for me that I am to use to establish Heaven on Earth.

I'll stop there. Hopefully, Reader, you can see the changes in my life and maybe you want what I'm starting to get. I wish at this stage I could tell you everything God put in my heart has played out perfectly but I can't.

I'm sharing with you *in real time as I go on this journey to pursue life how God intended.* With that being said, I can tell you I have been able to have a peace that nothing worldly can give me. I have fully recovered from drugs and porn. I am enjoying sex like

God planned. I do look forward to being a world-known example on what life according to God's laws looks like. Enough about me...

For this next part of the book, it's for Christians Only or people interested in Christianity Only. I say that because if you're not trying to live a life according to God's laws, you can fuck whoever you want.

Look at how society is changing as people are "exercising their options to have sex with whoever they want". This exercising of the sex-options has led to 2 dudes having butt-sex with each other and 2 females having fake sex with fake dicks. Again, this doesn't matter if you're not trying to follow God's laws, but there's a definite problem when the church is allowing people involved in homosexual activity to take the pulpit.

God's laws regarding sex aren't meant to damper our sexual experiences. In fact, He designed sex to be the ultimate experience for humans *within His guidelines.*

Sex is also designed to be practical and to be used to carry out His plans for humanity so homosexual and transexual activity fucks all that up. We humans are supposed to have sex between a man and a woman and have babies. Can 2 dudes having butt-sex use sex to make a baby? Can 2 chicks with a fake dick use sex to make a baby?

Sex like anything else in life needs to follow laws. God's laws on sex provide us with the most basic, common-sensest way to enjoy sex and be productive about it. As is the case, people are trying to use their sex-options to create laws that go against God's laws.

I think Canada has made it legal for you to have sex with an animal and not to single them out, I believe there are groups of people in the United States of America who are pushing legislation that would allow boys as young as 8 or 9 to have sex with grown-ass men. Then there are segments of American society who are pushing to teach kids that it's cool to get involved with homosexual and transexual activity.

All of these sex-options threaten to continue to make our society as mixed up and confused as ever and it doesn't have to be that way. We are seeing boys who think they can't be feminine and still be a boy. They're thinking they can "feel like a girl inside" and wear high heels and skirts. What's next for them? Are they gonna start wearing bras (with no titties) and maxi-pads (with no vagina)?

Am I being mean? Maybe, but if so, I'm not blaming the kids. I'm blaming the stupid-ass adults who are deciding to exercise their sex-options instead of following God's laws. More specifically, I'm mad at weak-ass Christians who 1) are allowing these types of sex-options to be practiced and applauded in society and 2) are involved with homosexual and transexual activity openly in the church.

If you'll notice, a couple paragraphs ago I said "threaten" to cause confusion and chaos in society. All of the nonsense that's been the result of a small group of people exercising their sex-options to promote homosexual and transexual activity won't win whatever fight they think they're fighting for and won't find whatever the fuck it is they're trying to find because in the end, like the Bible says, regardless of whatever options we humans use...God's way will prevail.

Am I saying anyone who is exercising homosexual or transexual options are evil and going to hell? No. I'm not privy to how Heaven and Hell works, BUT I do know, as a Christian who is sworn to uphold the laws of God, you are not supposed to exercise any sexual option that goes against God's laws.

Let's talk about tattoos. This seems to be something non-Christians love to point out with good reason. In the Bible, the author of Leviticus 19 records, "God says, do not cut yourself for the dead or put tattoo marks on your body..." (NIV translation). There are millions of Christians with tattoos and I am one of them.

Yes. Yes, I am guilty of exercising my "skin-option" and have tattoos on my chest, back, hands, arms and neck. Am I guilty of going against God's laws? Yes. Quick questions for you: By violating this law of God's, how confusing is it for society? By violating this law of God's, how many kids have become fatherless or come from broken homes? Do you see what I'm getting at? If not, let me explain...

Yes, as Christians we have ALL broken God's laws. Sometimes it was intentional and other times it wasn't. Sometimes we were guilty of exercising our options over God's laws and other times we may have been unaware of His laws in this area.

Ignorance of the law is not an excuse in the courts so I'm assuming that statement holds some kind of weight in the courts of Heaven as well. How that plays out, I don't know. I do know that once you and I as Christians are aware of God's laws, we are to follow them as best as we can.

In the case of tattoos, once I got serious about God and saw this law, I stopped exercising my skin-option and stopped putting tattoos on my skin. I don't even know why it's such a big deal, in fact, I think body art can be creative and cool, but then again: I don't need to know why God made that law…all I need to know is He made it and I need to follow it! I don't have any options now as it relates to tattoos.

I mean, it's easier to see that since God created a man and woman to use sex to create babies and have families, when 2 dudes are using sex for their own sexual pleasure, people are wearing condoms, taking birth-control pills, popping the morning-after pills or getting harmful devices implanted in their uteruses...those people aren't using their bodies the way God designed them to be used and that's obvious.

I have no ideal how having a tattoo is such a misuse of the body. There may be something I'm not seeing and like I said before, it's not for me to see. It's one of God's laws so any option I want to exercise that goes against His laws is a sin, a horrible option and something I have to steer clear of. Period.

This reminds me of a conversation I had with a friend of mine who is involved in homosexual activity. He said he basically had the option to be involved in that activity because, "...the Bible has so many rules and laws that nobody can follow them all. Plus, I respect God and just do the best I can. What about shrimp? Doesn't the Bible say you're not supposed to eat shrimp?"

You see, I told you earlier that people may not claim to be Christians, but they still have heard *something* about Christianity that made them either love it or hate it. In this case, my friend hates it because it goes against *his* options for what *he* wants to use sex for.

We didn't get into a big debate because that wasn't necessary. I do want to point out to you that yes, I am guilty of eating shrimp and yes, I am aware of the fact that God did say we weren't supposed to eat it...I'm also aware that Jesus came along and said part of this new covenant with humanity means that from now on, there is no unclean food because everything God made is good.

See how I was able to use the Bible and spin it so I could continue to exercise my food-option and eat chilled shrimp and dip 'em in cocktail sauce and not feel guilty? Be careful. Be very careful.

God's law is nothing to play with. Oh, I forgot to mention that I was going to ask my friend what act had more affect on society as a whole: him promoting homosexual activity or me eating shrimp, but that argument would have no true winner...

God's law. God's law is nothing to play with and Christians are just as guilty of playing with it and manipulating it to their advantage and that is part of the reason why non-Christians hate Christianity: the hypocrisy. Let's talk about hypocrisy so we're all on the same page...

What hypocrisy is NOT is somebody sharing what they've learned in life and are now showing others how to live a new way.

What hypocrisy IS is somebody sharing what they've learned in life and are now showing others how to live a new way...while they're still privately doing the exact activity they're telling other people they shouldn't be doing.

Many Christians, myself included, have painted a picture of Christianity that is undesirable and disgusting and it's no wonder that even though people around the world may have heard about Christianity aren't fuckin' with it and I don't blame 'em.

If you follow God's laws and not exercise our own options to do whatever we want, God promises us several beautiful, wonderful things. Here's a list of some of them:

1. I will make you a blessing to others wherever you go
2. Everything you touch will turn to gold
3. You will be in charge of entire cities
4. You will have a peace that the world can never take away from you
5. You will never know hunger
6. You will be protected from disease that hits everyone around you
7. You will have good health
8. You will be the lender and never the borrower

So, what do you think about that list? Is that a list that automatically makes you think: "Yeah! That list is a demonstration of how all the Christians I know are living!" Most likely not but that's okay. I have to repeat myself and tell you once again...do NOT throw the baby out with the bathwater!

God is telling you everything He wants to do for you and everything He can do for you and all you have to do to enjoy these blessings and benefits are follow His laws.

I know it seems hypocritical when you see billions of Christians who are crooked judges, business owners and politicians.

I know it seems like Christianity is full of shit when you see people worship the Pope more than they do God.

I know Christianity doesn't seem like a viable option when you see Christians who are singing spiritual songs, shouting out to God, crying because "God is so good to them" and praying to God for an hour or 2 on Sunday, and then the rest of the week they are singing songs with lyrics like, "Let them hoes fight!" and "Runnin' with the devil!", shouting at the driver next to them in a road-rage fit, crying because a wife left him because of his hidden porn and pill addictions and praying to God that, while he was out cheating on his wife, he didn't give her a sexually transmitted disease!

Here's the thing: even with all the negativity and lack of examples in the church and society on what a powerful Christian lifestyle looks like, hang in there! Just because us humans have fucked up, ignored God's laws and exercised our options in life to do things our own way does not take away from the power and effectiveness of God's laws.

Just because a law in society that is designed for good isn't working properly does NOT mean it's a bad law…it means there are people who are exercising the wrong options as it relates to the law. "Drinking and driving" is a good law, you just have people who can't handle their alcohol and aren't supposed to be behind the wheel of a car when they've been drinking.

Drinking alcohol, to some extent, is not a bad thing, just like driving is not in itself a bad thing BUT when you combine the 2, you have millions of drunk-driving, death-related injuries on record that could have easily been avoided by exercising different options.

God doesn't specifically say you can't drink. In fact, people who love to make fun of God love to point out how Jesus turned water into wine at a wedding. The truth is, even though God didn't say you can't drink, there are several instances throughout the Bible where people are warned about the dangers of drinking excessively AND we are told that our bodies "belong to God and are to be used for His purposes": it's hard to carry out His will while you're drunk, have an alcohol addiction or have a weak liver from drinking...

Options. Once again, as a Christian, you do have options but the option you choose HAS to be in line with His laws to the greatest extent you can. Fuck any of your options that directly go against His because there will be a zero-percent chance of a positive outcome for you.

Shit! I just realized I am basically giving you a summary of the book. The Summary Section is supposed to be a separate section, but here I am, caught up in the moment, giving you a Summary. Hmmmm, well, I guess this counts as the Summary Section.

So, Reader, I hope you will look seriously start to try and look at life through God's lens and not yours.

Exercise your option to follow His laws and be a good example of what life can really be like as a Christian. As a believer in all things God, the Bible and the Lost Books of the Bible.

Private Matter Bonus Essays

At the end of every Summary Section I have included some Private Matter Bonus Essays. These are essays I wrote that relate to the topic of the book and typically cover topics people only talk about in private. Check 'em out:

SALT and LIGHT

Salt and light are two of the most powerful and essential things on the planet. One has the ability to preserve things and the other has the power to expose things from fear to corruptions. Jesus said people who put His lessons into action should be the salt of the Earth and the light to the World. He wants His style of church to be a group of people with power and influence.

Jesus said the "Salt People" will be in charge of anything that deals with preserving the natural resources on Earth. Natural resources are not just steel, copper, plastic and water. It also includes human, animal and plant life. That means Salt People will need to do whatever they need to in order to hold any and all top positions that preserve the natural resources on Earth.

God instructed us to "maintain the Earth." This task ranges from recycling to protecting endangered wild life. It's not limited to those two tasks. They are just examples. The point is, God needs people who want to be the Salt to maintain and protect the Earth.

People who are destined to be the Light People have an equally important role. They will be tasked with exposing corruption in the world's systems. In general, light exposes things and acts as a guide. Whenever someone is in a dark place mentally, they need some type of light. Whenever a world system like finance and the media, are operating and getting wealthy based on corruption and things done in the dark, light needs to be shown on it to expose it.

Light People have the task of holding top positions of power in the world systems of finance, business, media, government, religion and education to keep corruption out. At the same time, Light People will need to be able to guide people who are in dark places mentally. Maybe by sharing their testimonies of how God brought them through dark times or maybe by becoming psychologists and therapists.

Your walk in life as a Salt Person or a Light Person will be ordained by God. What that process looks like will be different for each person. Maybe you will be both...

Just know that Jesus said there will be a lot of people out there who claim to want to follow Him...but the people who actually walk the walk and talk the talk will be few...

Be a part of the few, the proud. And yes, the Marines got that shit from Jesus.

ABORTION

Why is there such a big debate about abortion and when human life starts? This has got to be one of the stupidest debates in the world and that's why I don't get into that discussion. I may shoot off this Private Matter essay and that's about it.

Let me simplify a couple of key points for you:

1. **When does human life start?** Human life starts when a man and a woman have sex and she gets pregnant. Wasn't that simple? When a man and woman have sex and she gets pregnant, a human has started its' life. Oh wait, some of you may have been thinking that a man and a woman can have sex and create a whale? Or a horse? Maybe a rhinoceros? I mean, come on, people. Debating when a human life starts is a simple question and answer thing. We don't need the world's top "thinkers" to help

us in the discussion of when human life starts. There has to be more to it than just that...

2. **Is abortion 1st Degree murder?** Yes. Once again, pretty straight-forward here, people. If murder is when you make a plan to kill somebody and you carry it out...that's 1st Degree murder. Quick question for you: When you decided to kill the baby, was it planned out in anyway? Did you maybe call Planned Parenthood, give them your information, set up an appointment, got a reminder text the morning of, came in for the appointment and had the baby killed? If so, I'm gonna have to say that's 1st Degree murder. Here's another simple example for you: I get mad at a guy who stole my girlfriend. I know the bar where he likes to have a few drinks. He likes to get there at around 6pm and leaves around midnight. He doesn't live far from there, so he walks. I know his exact route. Just to make sure, I watch him for 3 nights. On the 4th night, I casually walk up behind him and quickly let off 2

shots, point-blank in the base of his head with a snub-nose, .38 Special and slowly slip into the car parked near the spot and my friends drives off. He's dead before he hits the ground. Everything works as planned. Is that 1st Degree murder? If it is, then abortion is murder.

3. **Is it the woman's right to kill the child?** Yes. Since the baby is inside the woman and she's the one who is going to start eating some pretty nasty food combinations, have her nose, feet, knees and ankles get swollen and sore…and let's not forget there will be something living inside her that will be growing, eating and shitting in her…I would *definitely* say she has the choice whether to let the baby human live or kill it.

Since the answers to these questions are extremely simple and straightforward, there has to be something behind the curtain when it deals with abortion. The key is to figure out what the fuck it is so we can stop wasting time with distractions and start using our efforts to enjoy life and stop killing it.

I'm going to suggest that it's a combination of guilt and Satan. I'll do the guilt part 1st because once you mention Satan, people don't know what to do or say. Is he real? Is he as bad as the Bible says? Does he really have the power to influence society? Getting back to the topic of guilt...

There is a growing trend in society to baby people. I'm not talking about little kids; I'm talking about treating grown-ass people like little kids.

The word "retard" means slow or slower. If there is a person whose brain is not developing at the rate it should to allow him or her to function as an adult, he or she is classified as being mentally retarded...not a "retard" or "retarded." See the difference?

One statement is a cold, by-the-book fact talking about a person's trait or characteristic; while the other is a label that takes away from a person's human value and is unacceptable for people to use...*especially* Believers.

How does this relate to abortion? When you pre-plan and carry out the death of an unborn baby, you are guilty of 1st Degree murder. That does NOT mean you are a murderer. It means you are a person who committed the crime of murder. Yes, you are guilty of that crime; but you are still a person who can 1) take responsibility for the crime of murder, 2) have the guilt aspect of it taken away and 3) you are not a bad, evil person.

People are trying to allow a mother-to-be to kill her child without the guilt. It doesn't work that way. Anyone guilty of a crime is guilty. A crime is a crime and guilt is guilt.

Let's talk about Satan and abortion. I will be brief because if you're interested in this topic more, you can read the book, "Safe Sex Saves Satan."

I do want to say Satan is a real being and it is proven that he hates humans. Why? Because he is a being who used to be one of the top-dogs in Heaven and got kicked out and can NEVER return to that blessed, powerful state of living.

His only goal now, and he put this on the public record for everyone to see, is to make sure humans don't get to enjoy Heaven on Earth or the spiritual realm known as Heaven. We are his eternal enemies.

What if...what if he *is* able to influence people? I mean, what if he was able to influence people to kill their babies? Wouldn't that help him accomplish his main goal?

Abortion serves Satan *extremely* well:

1. **Abortion kills humans. Every baby that gets murdered is one less human that can enjoy Heaven…just the way he wants it.**
2. **Abortion creates guilt. Every woman I know who has killed her growing baby has, on some level, had guilt. It's a natural reaction to have guilt after killing a baby. A female can say, "Yeah, girl. I just did what I had to do." Sounds good, but there's guilt. Anytime you live with guilt, it makes it hard for you to guide someone else in life. How can you tell your daughter to have responsible sex…when you had irresponsible sex that led to you killing a baby?**
3. **Abortion is a distraction. Do you know how much time and resources we waste on this abortion shit? How about we start focusing on responsible sex??? We do that and there's no more abortion!!**

Yes, I have been involved in abortions. 2 to be exact.

Yes, I have lived with the guilt of it and it makes me hesitant to tell my kids, or anybody for that matter, to have responsible sex...when I've had irresponsible sex that has led to the death of two babies.

Yes, I didn't feel right talking about responsible sex until I got into the Bible and allowed God to help me deal with the guilt of it all.

Oh! I just thought about something! Since abortion is 1st degree murder, shouldn't the person be charged with murder? Why isn't the mother and father charged with murder? If they are charged with murder, what should the punishment be? People get prison time for neglecting a dog or cat...so why shouldn't the parents get prison time? And if so, how far back can you go to charge somebody with the crime of abortion?

That's just something I had on my mind that I wanted to share publicly that a lot of us have talked about in private that needs to be discussed publicly.

LOVE LANGUAGE OF CHRISTIANS

I am married and me and my wife love God and we love sex. We like to fuck or make love. We don't like to have sexual intercourse. Does that mean we don't love God? Since we made sure we legalized our marriage in a church before God, does using the word "fuck" mean we have disrespected our sexual marriage vows to God? If we love God, does that mean we are supposed to use King James talk when it comes to bedroom talk? I don't believe so.

How are Christians supposed to talk when it comes to sex and love? That is a question that should be debated and discussed in the church. But the church doesn't know how to talk about it...so I will.

Before I was married, I used to tell females, "Yes, I want you to suck my dick." I NEVER said, "yes, I would like it if you put my penis in your mouth and receive oral sex from you." I NEVER just pulled my dick out and kind of smiled at her and looked from her mouth to my dick and back to her mouth hoping she would get the idea that I want my dick sucked. I openly said it then and now that I am married, I have to be just as open with her and vice versa.

If my wife just sat there with her legs open waiting for me to suck on her clit without a formal invitation...that shit ain't happenin'. She needs to feel free to express what she wants. I take that back. Actually, when you're married, there is a beautiful code you establish and nothing needs to be said. When I pull my dick out and lay back and smile at her, she knows what to do. When she lays with her legs open and raises her right eyebrow, I know what to do.

Now that I'm married, does that mean I can never say to my wife, "The kids are gone for the night, so you know we 'bout to get our fuck on all over the house. I want you to walk around naked so I can look at your sexxxy ass all day and when I can't take it anymore, I'm gonna grab you, turn you around, bend you over and fuck the shit out of you." Is that how married Christians are supposed to talk? Is that permissible Christian language?

Some of you may think I'm disgusting and that I am not a good Christian because I want to fuck my sexxxxy wife instead of wanting to "have sexual intercourse with my wife."

Some of you may think I'm disgusting and that I am not a good Christian because I want to lick my wife's pussy until she cums instead of wanting to "lick her in her clitoral/vaginal region until she reaches a climax."

Some of you may think I'm disgusting and that I am not a good Christian because I openly tell my wife to "turn around and put your ass in my face so I can kiss it. I think you have a sexxxy ass and I can't keep my mutha fuckin' lips and tongue off of that sexxxy thang" instead of openly telling my wife "Can you please turn around? I really like your buttocks and I would like it if you would bend over in front of me so I can kiss it. I just love the sight and feel of your rear end so much that I can't stop kissing all over it."

The point I am trying to make is that I don't believe you have to go all King James in the bedroom when you have sex as a Christian, married couple. God made sex to be enjoyable. One of the authors in the Bible said to the men, "get married to the woman you fall in love with as a youth and enjoy her breasts…" Another author in the Bible said, "the marriage bed is sacred and something for a husband and wife to enjoy however they see fit."

If that's really true, if my wife and I are used to talking a certain love language before we were married, we should feel free to talk in that same language as a married couple if that is the language that makes us comfortable, keeps our sex life strong and keeps us faithful to each other.

If I'm married and have sexual desires that I can't express to my wife, I am going to be inclined to hit the strip clubs and bars more frequently so I can come across a female who "understands" me and who I can enjoy having sex with. Since marriage is a thing that God supports and created as the power-base of society, we need to be talking about these things BEFORE marriage.

At the same time, there has to be boundaries and limits. Just because I may want to have anal sex with my wife does not mean she has to comply and take it every week in her ass. We still have to compromise. Maybe she takes it like that on Valentine's Day, President's Day and our anniversary or something. That's for you two to decide.

My point is that it's your marriage and your sex life. The point is, you two need to talk about sex or your marriage will fall the fuck apart. If you're a guy and secretly want to have sex with other guys, that's some shit your wife needs to know BEFORE you get married. We should all be at the point where we can share our views on sex and decide whether or not to move on together or get off the train.

Sex is an important element of marriage that needs to be talked about. When I look back at the people in my church when I was growing up, I can tell you that there was only one couple, and I won't say who it is, that looked like they were having sex. All the rest of the married couples looked like zombies. I never saw anybody sneak and hold hands or saw a couple share a laugh with another couple and the wife blush and kiss her husband on the cheek.

I went to an all-white church and that's what I saw. Anytime I went to white churches, that is the vibe I got. I have to go a step further and say I got the same vibe from all-black churches as well.

My experience with church and sex was that it never happened until...until somebody got a divorce because the wife was cheating or the husband had a full-blown porn addiction that was out of control.

There was a pastor who committed suicide because he was hooked on phone sex and spending hundreds of dollars a month. He felt guilty and felt like he couldn't share that with anybody.

Kirk Franklin, a famous gospel singer, came out and said he had a major porn addiction. He had porn videos stashed all around the house behind every television or something crazy like that. It happens. It happens to anybody and it needs to be talked about. It's major incidents like that when you realized people in the church had sex problems or were actually having sex.

I have to add this to be fair, Joel Osteen has a wife who looks like she wants to have fun sexually, she's attractive and dresses in a modern, conservative-yet-sexxxy style. That's refreshing to see.

Her husband Joel on the other hand, with his perfectly set and sprayed hair style, bleached white teeth with that permanent smile on his face and that joyful message he delivers every Sunday, looks like he could care less whether they had sex or not. I mean, they do have a couple of kids as proof, but other than that...you can tell Joe ain't really hittin' that like he's supposed to.

There is a twist to all of this. When I was in church, it was also the place where I saw plenty of sexxxxy females. An older friend of mine used to tell me that church was the best place to find a nice female. I think he must have been talking to a lot of church-going females as well because the single ladies in church had a tendency to dress sexxxy; unlike the married females who tended to want to leave the impression that they were sanctified, highly favored, blessed and content to be married.

It's unreal for us to think a pastor doesn't get turned on by females outside of his wife. If he didn't, that means he is either into homosexual activity (and should not be in the pulpit) or he is in complete denial of his maleness.

I've asked a couple preachers about this and even though they were married, they still say they see women as being attractive and even sexxxy. They even admitted to me that they still look at a sexxxy female walking by sometimes. For them though, they say the difference is their thought process: just because they are married doesn't mean they don't see or recognize female beauty...it just means they understand how serious marriage is and straying from his wife for some sex is not worth falling out of favor with God, destroying a marriage, destroying the power-base of the family structure, causing emotional harm to the kids and a bunch of other chaos that results from lacking sexual discipline.

If you think I'm being unrealistic, feel free to look around your church and see how many couples look like they are having fun sexually. Look at your pastor and his wife and see if you think he is hittin' it from the back and they are enjoying doing the reverse-cowgirl position or doing 69's.

When I look around congregations, I see plenty of sexxxy women I would like to have sex with (this of course is before I was married). What I don't see is married couples looking sexually satisfied; especially the pastor. Nine out of ten times the pastor's wife has a dress that drags down to her ankles and a shirt that's long-sleeved and buttoned all the way to the top button...looking like she walked straight off the television show Bonanza, Little House on the Prairie or some other old-school show.

Do I want my pastor's wife wearing short, sexxxy skirts with high heels and a short top so her ass shows? No. I'm not saying that. What I am saying is that when a person is having fun sexually, it shows in the way they walk, talk and dress and it would be nice to see a pastor-wife team looking like they are human and like they like sex.

In the end, I think, as one who was sexually irresponsible and a Christian for many years, that it's important that the church grow some balls and takes a stand on sexuality. Everybody else openly pushes their thoughts and agenda for sex.

People involved with homosexual activity have openly let it be known that they want to teach public school kids at early ages that homosexual activity is cool and it's something that has no negative or confusing impact on the family and society. Not cool. Very confusing.

The media has been pushing shows that send us the message that it's okay if you're a man and you feel like a woman...just cut your dick off, get a fake vagina, get some big, fake-ass titties sown onto your chest and BAM! YOU ARE NOW A LADY!!! Not.

It's time for somebody to stand up and start talking about the beauty of waiting to have sex until marriage.

It's time for somebody to stand up and start talking about how they did have sexual desires that went against the Bible and God, but they took the time to fight those feelings and not just fall victim to any and every sexual desire and urge that came their way.

It's time for somebody to stand up and start talking about the fact that getting fake titties doesn't make you a female any more than getting a fake dick sewn on your body makes you a man.

Whatever your view is it's important because it's your view. We may not all agree, but what we can agree on is the results. Start looking at the results of certain sexual behavior and see if it's a good thing or a bad thing. Doing this, I believe, will allow the natural design and order of sex to continue to be a beautiful thing.

It all starts with 1) your view on sex, 2) talking about sex and 3) making sex education an important topic in church, the home and schools.

THE ONLY HABIT YOU NEED TO SUCCEED

In order for any formula to be successful it must be able to be applied and used to anyone and any situation it was designed for. The formula for success is no different.

Nature provides us with many examples of true unbiased formulas. Look at the properties of water: if you take a glass of water and turn it sideways...water will run out. It doesn't matter if you are black, white, short, or tall, fat or skinny...it will always run out. I think you get my point without me having to go into examples of gravity, rain and evaporation.

Rules are essential for life. Everything about life is built around rules. Successful people know the rules and live by them...that is what makes them successful. Here's the problem: people try to change the rules for their benefit. Once that is done, that rule is no longer a valid rule. It's as useful as a pocket with holes in it.

Sporting activities have rules that seem to be the fairest. The process to get on a team or into an event may be manipulated, but once on the court or the field the rules apply to each player equally. There was a time in America when the entry process and the actual playing process was tainted and sports suffered as a result of it. Once the officials and prejudicial people hiding behind the scenes were able to see the benefit and rightfulness of applying the rules equally is when sports became the billion-dollar entertainment industries they are today.

Businesses that want to influence politics for their benefit use money to corrupt the rules. They pay politicians and legislators to create and pass legislation that favors their industry; often times regardless of the health hazards or resulting financial injustices that come from said legislation. We see this horrible, common practice applied in industries such as banking and sugar just to name a couple of guilty parties.

Rules are so essential that people will risk their honesty, their careers, spend millions of dollars and ignore their morality *just* to be able to bend the rules in their favor. That's because they understand that rules are what makes the world go round, and if they can manipulate the rules in their areas of interest, they will be "successful".

Here's the thing about rules: the best rules favor any and every one equally! The best rules are highly profitable and beneficial to all members in any given society! ANY type of manipulation in the process of creating or enforcing the rules will always have a negative effect and will be absolutely unproductive in the end.

Now we get to the part where you find out about this "one rule you need to succeed" thing. Well, drum roll please.......:

FOLLOW GOD'S LAWS IN THE BIBLE!

That's it and that's all. Following the rules in the Bible is your advantage in life. If there is a law that applies to one culture or economic class but not another...following God's laws will help you get through the corruption to get to your destiny. If there is a law that is designed to keep certain people out of an industry or acts as a glass ceiling...following God's laws will help you get through the corruption to get to your destiny.

The instructions in the Bible are extremely simple to follow and everyone has access to them 24/7...even without advanced education or training, WIFI or internet access. Here's how it works:

1. **Easy access**: God said "I will write these laws in their hearts and minds". Once you understand that all law and

order that comes naturally to you has a purpose and was placed inside you by the Creator of the universe...you can begin to understand that nobody is superior to you value wise. Someone may be a better athlete in a certain sport or better at accounting than you; but that only makes them more valuable than you in that particular arena...NOT IN LIFE.

Every one of us knows when we are doing something wrong. We somehow feel it inside that we are breaking some type of rule. The evidence is usually that the other person is sad or at a perceived disadvantage because of our actions. We can either change our actions or change the rules. The easy, corrupt way is to manipulate the rules so that we can continue to have a perceived advantage over someone else for our benefit. By making certain activities or actions "legal", people learn to justify the deception in their character by saying "well, it's legal." If ANY manmade law goes against God's Law it is NEVER going to be legal. I say "perceived" because any "advantage" that is forged out of trickery or deception isn't an advantage at all. In fact, it puts the deceptive ones at a disadvantage because they are living a life based on intentional lies and deception.

2. **The rules defined**: Jesus said the rules of life can be summed up by simply loving and respecting God and treating people how you want to be treated. How do you show that you love someone? You find out what makes them happy and you perform that act as much as possible.

God made this Earth specifically for humans so it doesn't make sense to think He doesn't love us! If He didn't love us, He would've made gravity 10x stronger than it is and we would all be dragging our feet on the ground, unable to walk or move. Plants that have stronger and healthier healing power than any medicine made or sold in the pharmaceutical markets would not exist if God didn't love us.

The other half of the "rule's equation" is treating people how you want to be treated. Would you want someone to tell you or your child that you can't go to a certain college because of your cultural group? Most likely not...so don't make those types of rules. The whole Civil Rights Era could have been avoided by following that one, simple Bible principle.

3. **The guaranteed path to success:** In the book of Genesis, God told Abraham "Because you obeyed me, I will make you great...your descendants will take possessions of the cities of their enemies..." God said He would help Abraham's descendants take over enemy territories and would make his name great. All Abraham did was obey what God told him to do. He did one major act to obey God and God made that huge promise to him.

When the Israelites were going to be led by God to their Promised Land, God said "In order to get there and enjoy everything life has to offer...all you have to do is obey my commands." He never said that you have to all get college degrees or come from certain backgrounds...simply follow His commands.

In the book of Joshua, we learn how Joshua's success in life was locked in. God told him "Obey my laws and you will have success wherever you go...no enemy will be able to stand against you...constantly think about these laws so that you can make good decisions..."

The word "enemy" is defined as: someone or something that tries to harm you or go against you. In the Bible, God was quick to let someone know that He would help them defeat their enemies. The enemies in these times were typically other countries that were at war with the Israelites or against any person that God supported.

I believe that same principle can be applied today to mean: anything or anyone who is against you or tries to harm you. That means if you obey God's laws that no type of legislation or rules that are deceptive in nature and meant to harm or be a stumbling block in your life will be successful.

4. **Summary of the only habit you need to succeed:** **OBEY GOD'S RULES.** Get into the Bible and apply any of the rules God gave. You can see the importance of rules and law and order in society, so follow the rules that give you the most freedom to enjoy life without encroaching on someone else's freedom to do

the same. In your industry, treat people how you want to be treated. Don't be a part of anything or anyone who supports laws that are contrary to the Bible. Focus on these laws habitually. Every day. Continue to understand and value your success and the proper way to get it. Understand that your personal value is not at stake but your personal level of success is. And as your success level in life rises, so does the success level of people around you.

EVERY SINGLE RULE IN THE BIBLE IS DESIGNED FOR YOUR HAPPINESS AND SUCCESS AND AS A WIN-WIN FOR EVERYONE AFFECTED BY ITS APPLICATION AND ENFORCEMENT!!

BIBLE: Basic Instructions Before Leaving Earth

HOMOSEXUAL ACTIVITY

I am against homosexual activity. Not because I don't like it. Not because I think it's weird. Not because I don't understand it...I am against homosexual activity because it goes against God's laws.

To be clear and fair, homosexual activity is only one of God's laws regarding sex that I am against. This may sound hypocritical, and people who are involved in homosexual activity or people who are against God, love to say that, but yes, I used to break all kinds of God's laws on sex.

God said we aren't supposed to cheat on our husbands or wives...I slept with a couple of married women in my day. That was wrong only because it went against God's laws and I had to stop. Did I want to stop? Not really, but I had no choice: it was either follow God's laws or my own laws.

God said we aren't supposed to lust. That means we aren't supposed to allow ourselves to see someone and view them as a piece of meat. I used to deal with that when I had a major porn addiction.

I would get high and watch porn for hours until my eyeballs dried up. I loved it. The rush of the endorphin releasing drug with the rush of the porn-visual had me hooked for years. I had to stop doing it. Did I want to stop? Not really, but I had no choice: it was either follow God's laws or my own laws.

People, particularly in the church, who love to point out the wrongs of homosexual activity, tend to forget about God's other laws surrounding sex. They like to point out homosexual activity while they themselves are lusting at strip clubs, hooked on porn or phone sex, cheating on their husband or wife or having sex with a very, very close family member.

This topic has been beaten up a lot and blown out of proportion. At this stage in the game, I understand 99% of humans are not involved in homosexual activity and 99% of humans don't understand homosexual activity and 99% of humans are scared to speak up and state their view because of media, personal, professional and social backlash.

I am not concerned with any of that, so I can speak freely. I follow God's laws as best as I can and I know He designed this place and that He runs shit, to if anybody has a problem with me stating my views…oh well. Get over it because I'm not stating my views, I'm stating God's views.

Anything I've done in the past that went against God's laws is something I have both an obligation to stop doing, openly confess what it is I was doing AND help people who are interested in following God's laws to stop as well. While we're on the homosexual subject, let's also be clear:

1. there is no such thing as homophobia or homophobic. People aren't scared of people who are involved in homosexual activity. That's a very effective term that people involved in homosexual activity have used to get their "opponents" to shut the fuck up, back down and let homosexual activity become a normal thing in society.

2. I don't call people involved in homosexual "homosexuals, gay, questioning, queer, bi-sexual, lesbian, stud, dike, fish, top or bottom" or whatever other labels are out there. I refuse to characterize someone by their sexual choices and preferences. If you like homosexual activity, you are simply a man or woman who likes homosexual activity.

3. I am not changing my basic understanding of the English language and start calling people "him/her/she/he." That's about the stupidest, dumbest thing I could ever do. It's not that I don't respect everyone's freedom of choice…it's simply because I know how to speak English and I know that "he" is a pronoun that describes a single, individual

male. There is enough changing of the English language with words like "bad", "shit" and "lit" meaning a thousand different things. I sure as fuck am not about to start calling "him" a "her" and "she" a "he" or "me" a "him/her/he/she."

4. Any State or country can legalize homosexual marriage, and any human who follow God's laws can *not* give a shit. I guess if a State says humans can marry animals that I, as a business owner, would have to start allowing spousal support for a German Shepherd's husband or wife that is an employee of mine? Get the fuck out of here. Won't happen. I operate along God's laws and am under His government's protection, guidance and care, so make whatever laws you want: if they go directly against God's laws, I will never follow them and you will never force me to.

In the end, do whatever *you* want. Suck on whoever *you* want. Fuck whoever *you* want. Marry whoever *you* want. Use fake dicks when *you* have fake sex if *you* want. Buy a fake vagina and have fake titties if *you* want…do whatever *you* want if *you* want to follow *your* own rules. When you want to wake up like I had to do and start following God's nice and easy rules for sex…let me know. I had to learn the hard way, but I might be able to help you switch over…if that's what you want.

Personal Development Notes

Personal Development Notes

Personal Development Notes

www.ingramcontent.com/pod-product-compliance
Lightning Source LLC
Chambersburg PA
CBHW050251220526
45465CB00002B/634